Escape to the
Paintbrush & Pencil

by Lesley Michele Hibbert

Dearheart Studio

www.dearheartstudio.co.uk

First published in the United Kingdom by Arc Publishing and Print 2021

ISBN: 978-1-906722-81-4

Hello and welcome to my new book. My hope is that this book is a gift to you or a treat to yourself. Turn the pages slowly reflecting on the different images. I'm not a professional artist or poet, I just appreciate the feeling of being creative, reflecting on life and inspiring others.

When my father died in 2012, he left me his art materials. I soon learned the importance of using good paper, much like in life, it's the foundation that needs to be strong and secure, add fresh water, a great choice of colours, a couple of brushes and voila you're on the journey of painting! I always remember the wise words of the well-known American artist Bob Ross who said 'there are no mistakes only happy accidents' I needed a few nudges to be creative again after so many years since school art classes. Those whispers lead me to build my Dearheart website and to attend a few fairs with my prints and short demonstrations.

I have been a healthcare professional for over 40 years and I'm grateful for my busy and rewarding role as a Mum too. I appreciate life and the journey of self-discovery, following passions, opportunities and trusting in the power of love, our greatest gift.

The pandemic has been an odd time for us all, so many people of all ages have had their world turned upside down. I have been able to work throughout, supporting our NHS to ensure many patients in urgent need are treat. The painting and poem about Koi carp was inspired by a busy day at work when you can observe people who know their role, they weave with their care and wisdom and skilfully dance in a random rhyme. In addition to this as a trained hypnotherapist I had the privilege to give guided meditations for staff who wanted some relaxing support, I feel even simple thoughts, concentrating on slowing the breath can have valuable benefits.

Sheffield is my home city, a green city built on a heritage of steel production and manufacturing. Sheffield has many parks and is surrounded by glorious countryside and the Peak District National Park. There can be nothing finer than getting out into nature to clear the head and enjoy fresh air and exercise. As you will discover many of my paintings are inspired by nature, thoughts and dreams. Escape to the paintbrush and pencil is a reflection of my light, I hope my enthusiasm to share this journey also inspires you to be creative and lights your way to shine brightly.

With Love and Light

Lesley

Butterfly

As I was sitting on the grass under the old oak tree;
A lovely, lively butterfly came down quite close to me,
He settled on a buttercup and sipped its nectar dew;
I gazed at the glow upon his wing,
Vibrant gold and peacock blue;
The flower swayed a tiny bit,
A little breeze went by;
He gave a wave then off he flew,
I lost him in the sky.

The beautiful and quite rare Monarch Butterfly sipping nectar from a thistle.

The Common Blue Butterfly, this female isn't quite as showy as the males.

Blue Butterfly

Flutter by butterfly;
Try to catch the light so high,
Let the sun shine upon your wing;
Smiling hugs and angels sing,
Lightning flashes, change of mind;
To steadfast, caring, peace and kind,
She rests upon the nettle;
Then plants a gentle kiss,
The nettle forms a buttercup;
And turns the song to bliss.

The Robin, voted the UK's favourite bird, this territorial toughie is loud and bossy but very endearing.

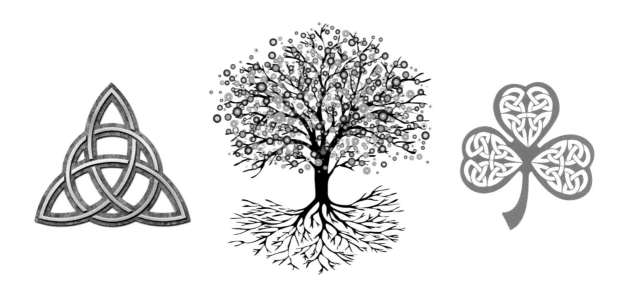

The Robin

She looked down upon his ruffled frame, the knowing gaze of calm acceptance as they rested together in the protection of the old deep rooted oak tree, a safe sanctuary of peace that evoked such powerful memories.
He looked like a young fledgling in eager pursuit of the next adventure.
Momentarily he was lost in her twinkling eyes before flying away, chirping merrily then pausing briefly to reflect.
A gentle breeze blessed with prayers of love and hope carried the busy robin as he circled the pink blue sky.
He would enjoy a fight and face bravely the storms as robins always do, protected by the kisses of his guardian angel planted on his chest.

Sunset dreaming or a magic portal, let your imagination flow.

A moment in nature

Be quiet, listen…. allow nature to speak in a multitude of ethereal sounds,
Breathe…..slowly… gently… smell the fragrance of the season, embrace the air around us.
Feel the grass damp with dew and the rough tree bark, hold nature respectfully in your
hand….its precious.
See natures simplicity and complexity, random surprises, magnificent colours,
intricate wonders.
Capture, reflect, etch the image on the inward eye.
Place peace and tranquillity securely into the crowded mind.
Imaginary thoughts gently meandering like a flowing spring gliding over
shiny pebbles.

Bamburgh Castle, Northumberland at sunrise in pastel crayon. From the A1 North turn off to Bamburgh, the magnificent sight of the 1400 year old royal fortress stands on a giant rock mound always takes my breath away, but don't tell anyone of this secret wonderful place.

Ladybower Reservoir in the Upper Derwent Valley. Created in 1945 and used in practice missions for the 617 squadron, as seen in the 1954 Dambusters film. Superb memorial flights take place with Lancaster and Spitfire planes.

Higger Tor a giant plateau of gritstone in the Peak District overlooking the Burbage Valley, Longshaw Estate and the Iron Age hill fort of Carl Walk.

Our beautiful Peak District edges, no wonder it's a climbers and hikers paradise.

Lindisfarne Priory, Northumberland. Holy island is cut off by a causeway at high tide. The priory was founded in 635 AD. The garden in the painting was designed by the famous Victorian plants woman Gertrude Jekyll, I added far more colour for my interpretation. The pre storm sky was just as shown!

Dreaming of the perfect beach holiday, sun, sea, surf.

Black over Bill's Mothers.
'If it's not raining it soon will be'.

Bluebell woods.
The incredible bluebells in May at
Renishaw Hall Gardens are a favourite.

Autumn walks, the autumn shades give that golden warmth before winter sets in.

The Starling

Alone he shone in iridescent hue;
Of bright lapis and sapphire blue,
His high pitched shrill, distinct and loud;
Certainly brought in such a crowd,
The mighty flock headed to the sky;
To keep together, to live or die,
Murmuring, synchronised, glide and swoon;
Gyrating forms on the autumn moon,
They soar to Earth and strive to Heaven;
Each bird observes its closest seven,
Grace and beauty in that single show;
Such wonder in their ebb and flow.

Migrating for the winter, many birds migrate to warmer climes but our Starlings welcome their cousins from the colder Eastern Europe, and join together to form the amazing murmuration in the sky. Sadly another bird in rapid decline due to pesticides.

Koi Carp.

Koi Carp

Swirling and twirling with iridescent shine;
A dance that dazzles in random rhyme,
The sinuous form glides and loops;
To deep dark depths this majesty swoops,
Crystal scales sparkle and capture his grace;
Confident alone or sharing his space,
Admiration and joy await at the light;
The symbolic koi carp now in my sight.

The Koi Carp symbolises good fortune, success, courage and good luck. We should all have one!

Sunset dreaming, wonder where the boat could go to?

2020

As 2020 comes to an end;
A year of change and not a friend,
We've adapted, cried, held our head in our hands;
Our plans delayed to far off lands,
Reflecting on our blessings and privilege we hold;
Thoughts of those less fortunate, hungry alone or cold,
Our Earth needs our care, to live simply without greed;
The planet will always grace us, we just need to plant the seed,
The wind of change is here, we've had warnings thick and fast;
Our globe has grown dark energies, and we've not seen the last,
Focus on doing good, raise the vibration way up high;
Chant, sing and beat those drums, eat chocolate and apple pie,
Our ego has been a burden, a chain to disrupt our soul;
Be free and observe nature, love and healing be your goal.

Springtime

The wonders of spring;
From birdsong to the fairy ring,
Listen to the merry tune;
The warmth of sun and bright full moon,
Hawthorn hedgerows, natures nest;
The hidden owl, an oak tree guest,
The secret door to higher mind;
A world to seek, to see, to find,
Tiny blue heads clump and dot;
The simple flower forget me not.

*Wood Warbler is one of the first singers in the dawn
chorus with the distinctive high pitched trill from such a tiny bird.*

The Gift

Drifting and floating down to the ground;
That special message that makes no sound,
Pure white and perfect heavens note;
Softly swooned like a spirit boat,
It came to rest in lumiere glow;
I pick the gift and gently blow,
Gratitude for that deep deep love;
A sacred sign from Gods own dove.

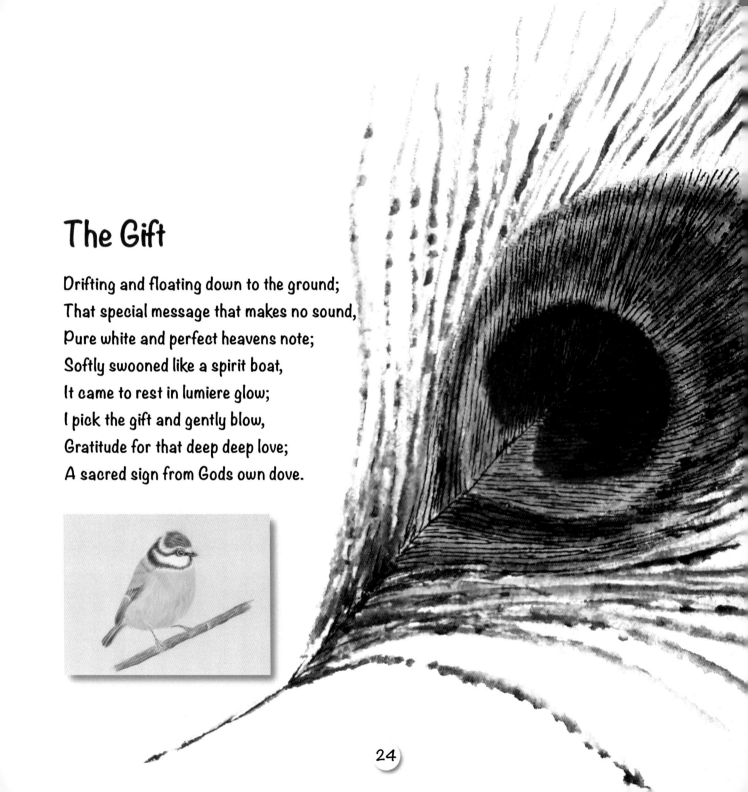

listen to understand and not to reply
whats meant for you wont pass you by

Easter

The Easter garden and bright blue sky;
Mistle thrush song, birds fly so high,
They busily make their nests with love;
From sparrows to the turtle dove,
Daffodils wave a bright smile to us all;
Notice, listen its natures call,
Capture the scene on the reflective eye;
To brighten a moment claimed by a sigh.

A Keepsake

The image shows a special place;

A room to rest your mind,

Thoughts may flow of family, friends and carers kind;

The light shines through a window of lilac and sparkling white,

This little gift sends love to you at a time that seems a fight.

Artwork by Celia Margaret. These keepsake cards are available for anyone who is going through a difficult time.

Phoenix emerging from the ashes, in bright acrylics. A motivational piece to 'Rise n Shine'!

The Prize

The sparkling prize;
That glitters the size,
Of vibrant light;
That beams out of sight,
The beacon in dark;
Charismatic gold spark,
Who shines to the end;
For loves ever friend,
The smile of pure grace;
That luminous face,
The hands point to pray;
From so far away,
So that peace will reign;
And love not wane,
Have faith, just be;
Belief is key.

Wonder

I've tried to tread the earth so lightly;
To bless the world to shine more brightly,
The simple smile, the hug, the kiss;
Who could enter the deep abyss,
The rainbow protection, the armour and sword;
Souls connected to a silver cord,
I wonder what the earth will bring;
To hopes and dreams that make us sing,
The story will unfold at last;
As planets collide to show our past,
When all of nature shout and cheer;
When souls unite and have no fear,
Open free, cleansed and new;
A peaceful world so kind and true.

My childhood teddy and friends sit together, though they mischievously push off tortoise when nobody is looking, this picture is called the fallen tortoise!

Pup and his favourite cushion to chew!

Venus

Secret Garden

Lady in waiting!

Venus

A scallop shell brought her;

She floated ashore,

Venus the Goddess for man to adore;

Produced by the foam,

Born of the sea;

For their heart and mind,

Only she had the key;

Venus with passion, faith and true love,

Find her, she's a blessing, the gift from above.

The lady with the lamp,
Not always seen, but
always there,
Lighting the way.

Be the light, shine from the heart.

Shine the light

The lady with the lamp, not always there,
But always lighting your way.

36

Village Ford with mother duck and ducklings.

This simple often over looked little flower, the Victorian symbol of true love and faithfulness.

Forget me not

'Don't forget me; said the forget me not;

I'm your love, not just a blue dot,

The resilient blue feast deserves an odd glance;

A delicate beauty to let your heart dance,

Moments of peace, a time just to ponder;

The striking blue flower that makes your heart wander,

Unnoticed until the sun is low;

A time to reflect and go with the flow,

That enduring blue glow is always around;

To love and behold that forget me not found.

Apple Tree

The apple tree, strong, brave and enduring,
Hidden roots of youth that grasp at stability from lifes fragility.
Nourished by sweet essences, memories of love
that fragrance the soul and lighten the heart.
The productive apple tree with entwining deep roots
at home in the orchard.

Apple Tree Cottage. I used to draw this little house from my imagination as a child.

Busy Bee

Busy bee, busy bee;
Working so relentlessly,
Flower to flower, site to site;
Only one can see the flight,
Settled on a buttercup;
Rests his weary head,
Peace at last in sunshine;
Pink skies and comfy bed.

Busy Bee, this is the common Carder Bee
enjoying a picnic.

Duckling

Calmly gliding across the lake;
Aware the pike a meal he'd make,
His busy feet flip and flap;
Duckling has no time to nap,
Ripples circle his fluid route;
His shrill quick quack is such a hoot,
She awaits, his tour, all but done;
With pride, success, achieved and won.

Shimmering reflections from the stream cast a silver glow on to the foliage around the waters' edge. A mother duck and her four precious ducklings weave and scurry through the tall reeds searching for food, alert to the greedy old pike who could easily devour one of her offspring. A hundred mayflies hover of the skin of the lake, airborne in loves passion until the end of their day.

Rainbow Wolf

The rainbow wolf
with transfixing eyes,
Deeply gaze
and mesmerise.

Wonder and wander;
No worry or race,
Slow gentle breaths;
A calm steady pace.

All creatures great and small

*Reindeer,
Santas transport.*

Field Mouse

*Rosie the black horse
shone blue in the
sunlight.*

Zebras from Yorkshire Wildlife Park.

The Dreamcatcher

There were still some apples on the tree;
One for horse and one for me,
But sitting by the tree that night;
I watched the full moon big and bright,
The dream catcher hung from the tree with care;
Aligned with the moon for a passing brown bear,
The moon shone through the intricate lace;
As the bears touched paws, the gentle embrace.

The Crucible and Lyceum theatres Sheffield, one of those rainy nights in pastel crayon.

The lake at Renishaw Hall, home of the Sitwell family for over 350 years.

Thornbury Hospital Sheffield, BMI/Circle Health group supporting the NHS.

Mums Page

My Mum, Edith was born in Worthing Road, Attercliffe Sheffield in 1920, in an area of heavy industry. It had a strong community with traditions like Monday washdays, whitewashing the step, blacking the grate. Mum had witnessed first-hand the Sheffield Blitz in 1940 from a shelter opposite Cockaynes Department Store. Seeing the flames and later the carnage left behind must have been terrifying. She joined the Royal Air Force as a WAAF during WW11 after working for Joseph Rodgers the cutlery manufacturer. Mum passed away in 2016, she had always remained stylish, vibrant, kind and an elegant shining light throughout her life.

~~The End~~

~~The Beginning~~

The Present ~ as the present is a Gift.